Demystifying Spanish Grammar

Clarifying the Written Accents, Ser/Estar, Para/Por, the Imperfect/Preterit, & the Dreaded Spanish Subjunctive

Brandon Simpson

Small Town Press
Dry Ridge, KY

D0754017

ACKNOWLEDGEMENTS

I would like to thank the following people for helping me:

Melissa Ibarra, professor of Spanish who reviewed the first draft of this book. I would also like to thank all my Spanish instructors and my Spanish-speaking friends for their contributions.

Matt Birkenhauer, professor of English, who edited my first two books.

Graham Stephen, fellow Spanish student, who helped me edit the final draft of this book.

ISBN: 978-0-9816466-0-2

www.BrandonSimpson.net

About the Author

Brandon Simpson has a Bachelor of Arts degree in Spanish. In addition to Spanish, he minored in French and has also studied other languages as a hobby. He is the author of *Learning Foreign Languages: Everything You Need To Know* and *If You Ain't Got No Grammer....*

Read more about him at **www.BrandonSimpson.net**.

DISCLAIMER

Neither the author nor the publisher can be held liable for the misuse of this book. The explanations herein are merely here to help your comprehension of Spanish grammar. Every possible effort was taken to ensure the accuracy of the information in this book. There may be, however, mistakes that neither the author nor the editors noticed. Some of the information in this book was provided by native speakers who are not necessarily experts of grammar. Reading this book will not guarantee mastery of the material nor will it guarantee a higher grade. This book is not endorsed by any company mentioned. The reader also should be aware that this book is not comprehensive. Readers should, and are also encouraged, to seek the advice of competent individuals.

Demystifying Spanish Grammar:
Clarifying the Written Accents, Ser/Estar, Para/Por, Imperfect/Preterit, and the
Dreaded Spanish Subjunctive

Table of Contents

Brandon Simpson

Chapter 1
Introduction

Why does this word have an accent?

When do I use *ser* and *estar*?

Why *por* and not *para*?

I don't understand the difference between the imperfect and the preterit.

The subjunctive? I give up!

Do these questions sound familiar to you? If they do, you have the right book. I had the same exact questions when I was studying Spanish. Now, I know them well enough to explain in this book. I have to admit that I don't always know the reason why I use one form instead of another; I learned a lot just from reading and listening to spoken Spanish.

As a Spanish tutor, I hear these questions all the time from struggling Spanish students. After I explain it to them my way, they say that they understand it much better. In fact, one of my students said that my explanations were clearer and more organized than the way the textbook explained it.

In this book I will attempt to demystify five grammatical structures. I will first show you my way, and afterwards I will show you other ways of learning it that other people have thought of. Before each *demystification,* I will explain why some methods of explaining these grammatical structures are problematic.

The first demystification deals with the written accents. Afterwards, the differences between *ser/estar*, *para/por*, and the *imperfect/preterit* will be demystified. And finally, chapters 6 and 7 deal with the dreaded Spanish subjunctive.

Having said all this, I must tell you that this book would

probably not be appropriate for beginning Spanish students unless you plan to study it intensively. This book is more for Spanish majors, Spanish minors, and anyone who is seriously trying to master Spanish.

Chapter 2
Demystifying the Written Accents in Spanish

Many Spanish students know where the written accents go, but they don't know why they go there. Others don't even write the accents because they don't think it makes a big difference; it does. One must write the accents because that's how the word is spelled.

In this chapter I have attempted to explain the rules for the accents with five basic rules. These rules probably don't encompass every possible reason, but they cover the majority.

Rule 1 For Accents-Stress

A word has a written accent if that word breaks a rule of stress in Spanish. The word *stress* simply means the syllable that is pronounced louder than the others. There are two rules of stress in Spanish. If the word ends in a vowel, an *n*, or an *s*, the second-to-last syllable is stressed.

Examples:
libro
hablan
casas

If the word ends in any consonant besides *n* or *s*, the last syllable is stressed.

Examples:
habl**ar**
com**er**
viv**ir**
habl**ad**
az**ul**

If a word breaks either of these two rules, the stressed syllable

15

must have a written accent over it.

Examples:
fácil
dif**í**cil
televisi**ón**
pel**í**cula
est**ás**

The word *fácil* ends in a consonant other than *n* or *s*, but the stressed syllable is not the last syllable but the second-to-last. So it must carry a written accent. The word *televisión* ends in a *n*, but since the last syllable is stressed, it must carry a written accent. If we make *televisión* plural and add *es*, it will have no written accent. Why? Look at the plural form: *televisiones*. The word ends in an *s* and the second-to-last syllable is stressed. So no written accent is necessary. The word *película* is accented on the third-to-last syllable. All words like *película* carry an accent. Spanish words are classified to four different categories of stress:

Last syllable is stressed - *aguda*
2nd-to-last syllable is stressed - *llana*
3rd-to-last syllable is stressed – *esdrújula*
4th-to-last syllable is stressed- *sobresdrújula*

Rule 2 For Accents-Monosyllabic Homonyms

Written accents also distinguish monosyllabic homonyms from one another. Monosyllabic means "one syllable," and homonyms are words that are spelled or sound similar to one another.

mi	my (possessive adj.)	mí	me (disjunctive pronoun)
el	the (def. art.)	él	he (pronoun)
de	from/of (preposition)	dé	form of *dar*
se	reflexive pronoun	sé	form of *saber*
si	if (conjunction)	sí	"yes"
mas	"but" (archaic form)	más	"more"

Fig. 2.1 (These words are written with accents to avoid ambiguity.)

Rule 3 For Accents-Diphthongs

The third function of the written accent is to separate two vowels that would otherwise create a diphthong. A diphthong is formed when two vowel sounds are pronounced at the same time and as one syllable. In Spanish, a diphthong must contain the letters *i* or *u*.

Possible Diphthongs in Spanish

ai- habláis	ia- hiato
ei- veinte	ie- hierro
oi- sois	io- criollo
ui- fui	iu-ciudad
au- jaula	ua-actuar
eu-deuda	ue-fue
ou- NA	uo-antiguo

Fig. 2.2

As you can see, all of these diphthongs contain the letters *i* or *u*. And when these vowels are combined with other vowels, they are pronounced as one syllable. If the word contains an *i* or a *u* that DOES NOT form a diphthong, there will be a written accent. And the written accent must be over the *i* or the *u*. (Note: The word *habláis* does not break the diphthong rule because the accent would have to be over the –i. In this case, the accent mark is over the *a* because, though the word ends in *s*, the last syllable is stressed).

Examples:
maíz
Raúl
continúa
avería
The written accent is on either the *i* or the *u*.

Rule 4 For Accents-Interrogative/Relative Pronouns

The fourth function of the written accent is to distinguish the meaning of the following pairs of words.

¿qué?	what?	que	that
¿dónde?	where?	donde	where
¿cuándo?	when?	cuando	when
¿cómo?	how?	como	like, as
¿quién?	who?	quien	who
¿cuánto(a)(s)?	how much/many?	cuanto(a)(s)	how much/many

Fig. 2.3

¿Cuándo vas a venir a casa?
When are you going to come home?

Voy a ir a casa cuando encuentre mis llaves.
I'm going to go home when I find my keys.

As you can see, a written accent is required in *cuándo* in the first sentence because it is an interrogative adverb. An accent is not required in the second sentence because *cuando* is used as a relative pronoun.

An accent is also required in indirect questions. Look at the following example:

No sé qué hacer. – I don't know what to do.

18

Rule 5 For Accents-Demonstrative Adjectives/Pronouns

The fifth role of the written accent is to distinguish demonstrative adjectives from demonstrative pronouns.

Demonstrative Adjectives

this/these

	Singular	Plural
Masc.	este	estos
Fem.	esta	estas

Fig. 2.4

that/those

	Singular	Plural
Masc.	ese	esos
Fem.	esa	esas

Fig. 2.5

that/ those over there

	Singular	Plural
Masc.	aquel	aquellos
Fem.	aquella	aquellas

Fig. 2.6

Demonstrative Pronouns

this/these one(s)

	Singular	Plural
Masc.	éste	éstos
Fem.	ésta	éstas

Fig. 2.7

that/those one(s)

	Singular	Plural
Masc.	ése	ésos
Fem.	ésa	ésas

Fig. 2.8

that/ those one(s) over there

	Singular	Plural
Masc.	aquél	aquéllos
Fem.	aquélla	aquéllas

Fig. 2.9

Look at the following two sentences:

Me gusta esta camisa roja.
I like this red shirt.

Me gusta ésta.
I like this one.

In the first sentence, *esta* is used as an adjective whereas in the second it is used as a pronoun: *ésta.*

The Diéresis

Another graphic mark used in Spanish is called the *diéresis*. The *diéresis* is simply two dots over the vowel *u*. And it only occurs over the *u* unless you're reading Old Spanish literature. This mark is also called *le tréma* in French and an *umlaut* in German.

The *diéresis* is written over the *u* before an *e* or an *i* to tell the reader that the *u* is pronounced in that particular word. It always appears in the combinations *güi* (gwi) or *güe* (gwe). If the *u* lacks the *diéresis*, the *u* is not pronounced and simply tells the reader that the –g is hard. For example, the combination *ge* is pronounced (xe/he), e.g. *geología*. This is the soft sound. If the word had a hard *g* sound, there would be a *u* after it: *gue* (ge), e.g.

20

guerra. But the *u* is not pronounced in this case. If a word has a pronounced *u*, there must be a *diéresis* over it.

> Examples:
> lingüista
> lingüística
> bilingüe
> güero

Exercise 1
Choose the correct word in the following sentences.

1. ¿Que/qué hora es?

2. Tiene algo para mi/mí.

3. Necesito el/él libro.

4. Mi hermano no quiere este/éste carro.

5. ¿De donde/dónde eres?

6. ¿Cual/cuál es la capital de México?

7. Uno debería aprender una lengua como/cómo la aprenden los niños.

8. ¿Como/cómo te llamas?

9. ¿Cuantos/cuántos años tienes?

10. ¿Quien/quién es usted?

Exercise 2
The following passage doesn't have any written accents, *diéresis*, or tildes (~). Fill them in.

Me llamo Marcos de la Vega. Soy de Espana. Tengo dieciseis anos. Este semestre estudio la literatura espanola, ingles, frances, matematicas, geologia y biologia. Me interesan muchos las lenguas extranjeras. Cuando vaya a la universidad, me gustaria estudiar la linguistica. La linguistica sera facil para mi puesto que soy multilingue.

Tengo dos hermanos. Viven en Mexico. Mi hermano Juan tiene veintidos anos y tiene un nino. El tiene dos anos. A el y su mujer les gustaria tener mas ninos en el futuro. Mi otro hermano Miguel tiene veinte anos y vive en el Peru. Ambos mis hermanos son bilingues. Hablan espanol e ingles.

Typing the Accents on Your Computer

The following are codes that you can use to type the written accents, the tilde over the ñ, the *diéresis*, and the upside down question and exclamation marks. (These work for PCs.)

ALT + 0225 á	ALT + 0201 É
ALT + 0233 é	ALT + 0205 Í
ALT + 0237 í	ALT + 0211 Ó
ALT + 0243 ó	ALT + 0218 Ú
ALT + 0250 ú	ALT + 0220 Ü
ALT + 0252 ü	ALT + 0209 Ñ
ALT + 0241 ñ	ALT + 0191 ¿
ALT + 0193 Á	ALT + 0161 ¡

This concludes this summary of the rules for the written accents. These are not the official rules. They are simply rules based on my observation. If you want to read about the official rules, you should consult *Spanish Pronunciation: Theory and Practice* by John Dalbor. The rules are in chapter 31, and the section is called *Rules for Written Accents in Spanish* (290-293).

Chapter 3
Demystifying *Ser* and *Estar*

Ser and *estar* both mean *to be*. "*Ser* is permanent, and *estar* is temporary." That's probably how you learned the differences from many of your Spanish grammar books, but unfortunately this explanation is very flawed. For one thing, *estar* does not always express temporary conditions. For example, if you wanted to say "I'm a student," what would you say? Based on the above definition of *ser* and *estar*, you would probably say "Yo estoy estudiante." Being a student is temporary, right? But this sentence is wrong. One must say "Yo soy estudiante." To properly learn how to use *ser* and *estar*, you need to forget the above definition; it is very problematic.

Another explanation is this: *ser* denotes the "nature/essence of being," and *estar* denotes the "state of being." I've heard this from several teachers, but I think it's too vague.

In their book *Spanish Verbs: Ser and Estar*, Juan and Susan Serrano say that *ser* is used for "WHATNESS" and that *estar* is used for "HOWNESS" and "WHERENESS" (Serrano & Serrano, 19). This definition is more straightforward than the "nature vs. state" explanation, but it's still a little too vague. Their book is very comprehensive and contains many examples.

When I explain *ser/estar* to students, I use acronyms. **JETCO** is for *ser*, and **LET** is for *estar*.

ser

Jobs/Identification Statements
Event location
Telling time
Characteristics
Origin/nationality

estar

Location (not event)
Emotions
Temporary feelings

Conjugation of *ser* in the present tense

soy	somos
eres	sois
es	son

Fig. 3.1

Conjugation of *estar* in the present tense

estoy	estamos
estás	estáis
está	están

Fig. 3.2

Examples of *ser*:
1. Yo soy cocinero. – I'm a cook. (job)
2. La reunión es en la sala 500. – The meeting is in room 500. (event location)
3. Son las dos de la mañana. – It's 2 o'clock in the morning. (telling time)
4. El profesor es alto. – The professor is tall. (characteristics)
5. El nuevo estudiante es de España. – The new student is from Spain. (origin)

Examples of *estar*:

1. Madrid está en España. – Madrid is in Spain. (location [not event])
2. Mamá está enojada. – Mom is angry. (emotions/feelings)
3. El hombre está borracho. – The man is drunk. (temporary feeling)

Problematic Adjectives

There are a few problematic adjectives for Spanish students. The most common ones are *gordo (fat)* and *delgado (thin)*. English speakers assume that *estar* is used because they think that being fat or thin are temporary conditions. This is not the case. They are characteristics that one EXPECTS to see in somebody. If Juan is fat today, we EXPECT to see him fat tomorrow and next week. Therefore, *ser* is used with these adjectives and any synonym of them.

Variable Adjectives (Adjectives that Change Meaning)

Many adjectives change meaning when they are used with *ser/estar*. The most common example used is probably the adjective *aburrido*. When it is used with *ser*, it means *boring*. When it is used with *estar*, it means *bored*. Below is a list of the most commonly used variable adjectives.

Adjective	ser	estar
aburrido	boring	bored
bajo	short	low
alto	tall	high
borracho	alcoholic	drunk
enfermo	terminally ill	sick
muerto	stiff	dead
listo	bright (intelligent)	ready
seguro	secure/safe	sure

Fig. 3.3

Another thing that varies with *ser/estar* is when you use it with the interrogative adverb *¿cómo?* When *ser* is used with *cómo*, it means that the speaker is asking about a characteristic. When *estar* is used with *cómo*, it means that the speaker is asking how someone is feeling or doing.

¿Como eres? – What are you like?
¿Cómo estás? – How are you?

Choose the correct verb in the following sentences.

1. ¿Qué hora es/está?
2. Soy/estoy enfermo.
3. Mi hermano es/está estudiante.
4. Mis primos son/están de Inglaterra.
5. La fiesta es/está en la casa de Juan.
6. George Bush es/está republicano.
7. ¿Dónde es/está tu carro?
8. Mi hermanito es/está muy bajo.
9. La temperatura es/está muy baja hoy.
10. ¿De dónde eres/estás?
11. Ese hombre es/está muy gordo.
12. Aquellas chicas son/están muy flacas, ¿no?

Fill in the blank with the correct form of *ser* or *estar*.

1. Yo _____ muy cansado.
2. La profesora _____ muy inteligente.
3. Nosotros _____ de México.
4. _____ las dos de la tarde.
5. Arnold Schwarzenegger _____ el gobernador de California.
6. Mi padre _____ enojado conmigo.
7. ¿Qué hora _____?
8. La reunión _____ aquí en dos horas.
9. París _____ en Francia.
10. ¿Cómo _____ tú?
11. Ese hombre _____ borracho.
12. La nieve _____ blanca.

Translate the following sentences.

1. I am drunk.
2. That man is an alcoholic.
3. This price is really high.

4. My son is tall.
5. It is 3 o'clock.
6. My mom is a teacher.
7. Our dog is small.
8. Where is the meeting?
9. His friend is Mexican.
10. Her friend is from Spain.
11. San Juan is in Puerto Rico.
12. My girlfriend is very happy.

Other Uses of ser/estar

Ser is also used to form the passive voice. But since it is more common to use the passive voice when *ser* is used in a past tense, it will be explained in chapter 5. Even then it is less common than the active voice.

Estar is used to form the progressive tenses. The progressive tenses are similar to English. In English one uses a conjugated form of the verb *to be* plus the present participle. The present participle is the *ing* form of a verb. Although the use of the progressive tenses is less common in Spanish, they are still used on a regular basis.

Example:
I am singing. - Yo estoy cantando.

The present progressive in Spanish will be explained here. To form the present progressive one takes the present tense of *estar* and adds the present participle of the main verb. For *ar* verbs, remove the *ar* and add *ando*. For *er* and *ir* verbs, remove the *er/ir* and add *iendo*.

-ar	-ando
-er	-iendo
-ir	-iendo

Fig. 3.4

Examples:
1. Estoy cantando. - I'm singing.
2. Estamos comiendo. - We're eating.
3. Ella está saliendo. - She's leaving.

Tener

Sometimes Spanish uses the verb *tener* when *to be* is used in English. It is used in the expressions *tener* _____ *años, tener calor,* and *tener frío.*

Examples:
Yo tengo 22 dos años. (Don't forget the ~ over the 'n'.) - I am 22 years old.
Ella tiene calor. - She is hot.
Ella tiene frío. - She is cold.

Ser can be followed by an adjective, a noun, or a past participle. It can never be followed by an adverb. *Estar* can be followed by an adjective, an adverb, or a present participle. It can never be followed by a noun.

To further understand the differences between *ser* and *estar*, consult *Spanish Verbs: Ser and Estar* by Juan and Susan Serrano. As you can see from this chapter, the "permanent vs. temporary" rule does not work. It is best to memorize the acronyms JETCO and LET to remember the differences between *ser* and *estar*.

Chapter 4
Demystifying *Para* and *Por*

A beginning Spanish student asked me what the difference was between *para* and *por*. I couldn't tell her because I honestly didn't know the rules. I just *knew* when to use them from experience. But this explanation wouldn't be helpful to anybody. So I thought about the differences, read some rules, and helped other students. Eventually, I figured out a set of rules that demystified *para* and *por*.

These two prepositions are usually translated as *for* in English. But they cannot be used interchangeably. Usually one must use one or the other. If both can be used, the meaning changes as well.

para
1. Destination (movement towards)
2. Deadline
3. Recipient
4. Purpose

por
1. Movement through
2. Duration
3. Replacement (in exchange for)
4. Reason

When *para* precedes a place or location, it means *towards*.
Example:
Viajo para España. - I'm traveling to (towards) Spain.

When *por* precedes a place a location, it means *through*.
Example:
Viajo por España.- I'm traveling through Spain.

When *para* precedes a date or time, it means *by*.
Example:
Hay que entregar el trabajo para el dos de mayo. - The work is due by the second of May.

When *por* precedes a date or time, it means *during*.
Example:
Siempre estudio por dos horas . - I always study for two hours.

Para is used before a recipient.
Example:
Tengo algo para ti. - I have something for you.

Por is used when something is being exchanged.
Example:
Pagué mil dólares por mi carro. - I paid a thousand dollars for my car.

One of the students I tutored was confused when she read the explanation of *para/por* in her textbook. It said that *por* + *person* means *for the sake of*. This definition was very unclear; it made *para* and *por* look almost the same. So I used to following sentences to clarify the definition.

Yo trabajo para usted. - I work for you. (recipient: as in you are my boss)
Yo trabajo por usted. - I work for you (replacement: I'm taking your place.)

Purpose vs. Reason

Para expresses purpose (or a goal) while *por* reason. Purpose indicates a future intention, and reason indicates a pre-existing problem/situation.
One of the first uses of *para* that Spanish students learn is

this: *para* + INFINITIVE=in order to + VERB.
    Example:
    Estudio para aprender. - I study in order to learn.
The purpose of studying is to learn. Learning is the future intention. Most students learn the expression *para* + *infinitive* in elementary Spanish.

    Para can also be used in the conjunction *para que* which means *so that*.
    Example:
    Estudio mucho para que mi nota sea mejor. - I study a lot so that my grade will be better.

    The purpose of studying is to get a better grade. Getting a better grade is the future intention.
    I can remember at least one problematic expression that involved *para/por* from my Spanish class: *to study for an exam=estudiar para un examen*. Most of my fellow students thought that *por* should be used here because *por* expresses that the reason of studying is the test: to study because of the exam. But this is not the case. *Para* is used because the *purpose* of studying is the exam; the exam takes place in the future. Our professor tried to explain that the exam was the recipient of the studying, but this didn't make any sense to the class. So I pondered this expression until I figured out the purpose/reason explanation.
    ¿Por qué? means *Why?* as in *¿Por qué estudias español?* (Why do study Spanish?) *¿Para qué?* means *What for?* as in *¿Para qué estudias español?* (What do you study Spanish for?) To most English speakers these two questions sound similar, but they are not.
¿Para qué? means *For what purpose?*, and *¿Por qué?* means *For what reason?*

    1. Purpose
    ¿Para qué estudias español? - For what purpose do study Spanish?

Possible responses:
>Estudio español para viajar en países hispanohablantes.
>Estudio español para mejorar mi CV.
>Estudio español para comunicar con mis clientes de México.
>Estudio español para que mis clientes hispanohablantes me entiendan.
>Estudio español para que las universidades me acepten.

2. Reason
¿Por qué estudias español? - For what reason do study Spanish?
Possible responses:
>Estudio español porque es obligatorio.
>Estudio español porque es una lengua bonita.
>Estudio español porque mi novia es de España.

¿Para qué? - For what purpose?
¿Por qué? - For what reason?
para que - so that
porque - because

The first question asks what the purpose of studying Spanish is, so the question is asking what the future intention is. And all of the possible responses are future intentions. The second question asks what the reason for studying is, which implies that there must be a pre-existing problem/situation/fact. All of the possible responses imply a pre-existing problem/situation/fact.

Other Uses of por and para

Por is also used in fixed expressions like *por favor, por ciento, por casualidad,* etc. It is also used in mathematics: *dos por dos=two times two. Por* is also used in the passive voice and translates into *by.*

> Example
> *El hombre fue mordido por el perro.*
> *The man was bitten by the dog.*

Por also means *on behalf of* as in *votar por* which literally means *to vote on behalf of.*

> Example
> *Yo voté por él.*
> *I voted for (on behalf of) him.*

Por is also used before locations in which case the meaning is *around.* The most common expression of this type is *por aquí* (*around here*).

Por is also used when its object is a medium which means "by means of."

> Example
> *Viajamos por avión.*
> *We traveled by (means of) plane.*

Para is also used when speaking about opinions.

> Example
> *Para mí, el español es fácil.*
> *For me, Spanish is easy.*

Choose *para* or *por* in the following sentences.

1. Estudio mucho _____ conseguir una buena nota.
2. Anduvimos _____ la calle.
3. Cuatro _____ cuatro son dieciséis.
4. Viajamos _____ España.

5. El libro fue escrito ____ Nebrija.

6. Los estudiantes estudiaron ____ dos horas.

7. Me gustaría un café, ____ favor.

8. Noventa ____ ciento de la clase entiende la lección.

9. Aprendo francés ____ que mis clientes francófonos me comprendan.

10. Aprendo francés ____ que mis clientes francófonos no hablan mucho inglés.

11. La tarea es ____ las dos de la tarde el 2 de mayo.

12. Este regalo es ____ mi hijo.

13. Tengo que estudiar ____ el examen.

14. ____ casualidad, ¿sabes la hora?

15. Voy a trabajar ____ el Señor Jaime.

16. ¿____ quién votaste?

17. ¿Cuál es más fácil ____ ti?

18. ____ un japonés, habla inglés muy bien.

Translate the following sentences. Each sentence requires *para* or *por*.

1. My son studies Spanish because he wants to improve his CV.

2. School was canceled because of the weather.

3. We went to Spain.

4. We traveled through Spain.

5. I need to study for the exam.

6. The girl watched TV for three hours.

7. Three times three is nine.

8. Five is fifty per cent of ten.

9. The homework is due on Friday.

10. I have something for you.

Para/Por Can Both Be Used

There is at least one case where both *para* and *por* can be used interchangeably without changing the meaning: *estar para/por* + INFINITIVE. This means *to be about to.*

Examples:
Estoy para comer. - I'm about to eat.
Estoy por comer. - I'm about to eat.

One of my Spanish grammar books say that these two sentences are not the same, but a native speaker told me that there is no difference.

Para is used to express "movement towards," deadlines, purpose, recipients and opinions. *Por* is used to express "movement through," duration, reason, replacement, "by means of," "per," quantity, and fixed expressions.

Chapter 5
Demystifying the Imperfect and the Preterit

Most Spanish students know how to conjugate these two tenses, but they always have trouble deciding which one to use because they both convey past actions. Almost every book on Spanish will tell you the following explanation or something similar: the imperfect is used for incomplete actions, and the preterit is used for complete actions. This is true, but it's a little too vague. When I tutor students, I use the acronyms **HIDE** and **STARS**.

Although most students don't have a problem with conjugating these tenses, verb tables will be shown here for your convenience.

For the imperfect of *ar* verbs, remove the *ar* and add the appropriate endings.

hablar

	Singular	Plural
1	habl*aba*	habl*ábamos*
2	habl*abas*	habl*abais*
3	habl*aba*	habl*aban*

Fig. 5.1

For the imperfect of *er* and *ir* verbs, remove the ending and add the appropriate endings.

comer

	Singular	Plural
1	com*ía*	com*íamos*
2	com*ías*	com*íais*
3	com*ía*	com*ían*

Fig. 5.2

37

vivir

	Singular	Plural
1	viv*ía*	viv*íamos*
2	viv*ías*	viv*íais*
3	viv*ía*	viv*ían*

Fig. 5.3

There are only three irregular verbs in the imperfect. They are *ser, ir,* and *ver*.

ser

	Singular	Plural
1	era	éramos
2	eras	erais
3	era	eran

Fig. 5.4

ir

	Singular	Plural
1	iba	íbamos
2	ibas	ibais
3	iba	iban

Fig. 5.5

ver

	Singular	Plural
1	veía	veíamos
2	veías	veíais
3	veía	veían

Fig. 5.6

*It could be said that these three verbs are regular. The endings are the same. The stems are irregular.

To learn the uses of the imperfect, use the acronym **HIDE**.

Habitual actions (used to + verb)
Incomplete actions (was/were + ing form of verb)
Descriptions in the past
Emotions/feelings

Whenever English uses the habitual past (used to + verb), Spanish uses the imperfect. This rule, however, has a few exceptions. Whenever English uses the past progressive (was/were + *ing* form of verb), Spanish ALWAYS uses the imperfect. The imperfect is also used to describe things in the past, and it is used when expressing one's emotions. Many Spanish grammar books say that the imperfect is used when something happens repeatedly, but this is a flawed explanation. If you said "Leí este libro," it would require the preterit. According to the flawed explanation, you would have to say "Leía este libro dos veces" if you wanted to say "I read this book twice." However, this is incorrect. It should be "Leí este libro dos veces." When those grammar books say that the imperfect is used for actions that happen repeatedly, they mean to say that it is used for habitual actions (used to + verb).

Examples of imperfect:
Siempre iba al cine cuando yo era joven.
I always went to the movies when I was young.

Ella hablaba en francés.
She was speaking in French.

Su carro era blanco y solamente tenía tres llantas.
His car was white and only had three tires.

No me sentía bien.
I didn't feel well.

Conjugating the preterit:

For *ar* verbs, remove the *ar* and add the appropriate endings.

hablar

	Singular	Plural
1	hablé	habl*amos*
2	habl*aste*	habl*asteis*
3	habl*ó*	habl*aron*

Fig. 5.7

For *er* and *ir* verbs, remove the *er/-ir* and add the appropriate endings.

comer

	Singular	Plural
1	com*í*	com*imos*
2	com*iste*	com*isteis*
3	com*ió*	com*ieron*

Fig. 5.8

vivir

	Singular	Plural
1	viv*í*	viv*imos*
2	viv*iste*	viv*isteis*
3	viv*ió*	viv*ieron*

Fig. 5.9

There are many irregular verbs in the preterit. You should consult a verb book like *Barron's Spanish Verbs* or *The Big Red Book of 555 Spanish Verbs* if you need to look up a conjugation.

To learn the uses of the preterit, use the acronym **STARS**.

Sudden occurrence
Time limit/Completed Action
Action disrupts the action of the verb in the imperfect
Reaction to another action
Series of distinct instances

As you can see, all of these fall under the category of "complete action" if we return to our initial explanation of the preterit. But it helps to have clarifications like this.

Examples of the preterit:
Empezó a llover.
It started to rain.
(Sudden occurence, complete action)

Llovió por dos horas.
It rained for two hours.
(time limit)

Yo estudiaba cuando sonó el teléfono.
I was studying when the phone rang.
(action disrupts the action of imperfect verb)

Cuando mi hermano usó mis zapatos, me enojé.
When my brother wore my shoes, I got mad.
(reaction to another action)

Leí este libro dos veces.
I read this book twice.
(series of distinct instances)

Decide whether to use the imperfect or the preterit in the following sentences. Afterwards, translate them into Spanish.

1. It was raining.

2. I saw my teacher.

3. I was reading a book when I saw a cat.

4. She read this book three times.

5. They didn't come because they were tired.

6. We used to go to the movies all the time.

7. What were you doing?

8. What did you do?

9. It rained for three hours.

10. The house was small and white.

11. I ate there every day.

12. What did you eat?

13. What were you eating?

14. The man was singing in French.

15. The man sang in French.

Aspect

Another way of explaining the differences between the imperfect and the preterit is using the concept of aspect. Imperfective aspect expresses incomplete actions, and perfective aspect expresses complete actions. This is really just a fancy explanation of the definition explained in the beginning of the chapter.

Imperfective=Incomplete=Imperfect
Perfective=Complete=Preterit

If you ever read *Gramática de la lengua castellana* by Antonio Nebrija, you will notice that Nebrija named the imperfect tense "el pasado no acabado" and the preterit "el pasado acabado."

Pasado no acabado=Unfinished past=Imperfect
Pasado acabado=Finished past=Preterit

"What was going on?"/ "What happened?

If the acronyms HIDE and STARS do not work for you, you can ask yourself if the situation you are talking about answers the question *What was going on?* (imperfect) or the question *What happened?* (preterit). This is good if the situation cannot be explained in the above rules. For example, if you wanted to say "The cat was eating," you would immediately know that the imperfect is required because this is an incomplete action (was/were + ing form). But you can also ask yourself if this situation answers one of the above mentioned questions. This situation answers the question *What was going on?*, but it does not answer the question *What happened?* The translation, therefore, is "El gato comía."

Another example is the following sentence: "¿Qué (era/fue) lo más divertido de tu año en Ecuador?" The HIDE/STARS acronyms don't work very well here. So we can ask ourselves if the situation answers the question *What was going on?* or *What happened?* This sentence answers the question *What happened?* Therefore, we know to use *fue*.

Imperfect Progressive/Preterit Progressive

These two progressive tenses both require the verb *estar* in either the imperfect or the preterit with the present participle of the main verb. These two tenses have very subtle differences. Read the following two sentences.

Yo estaba leyendo un libro. – I was reading a book.

Yo estuve leyendo un libro. – I was reading a book.

They both translate into the same sentence in English, but there is a very subtle difference between them. The first sentence indicates that the speaker was reading a book without interruption. The second indicates that the speaker was reading a book with interruption. To avoid ambiguity one should add something to the second sentence like a time frame.

Yo estuve leyendo un libro hasta la medianoche.
I was reading a book until midnight.

If you add a time frame like *hasta la medianoche*, the preterit progressive is required. But you can avoid both of these tenses by using the imperfect. It will work in both cases.

Habitual Past

Some English speakers wonder how Spanish speakers know when they are talking about a habitual action or a past action in progress if they use the same tense for both. You can use the imperfect progressive for "was/were + ing form." This can never mean "used to + verb." If you want to clarify that you mean "used to + verb," use the imperfect of the verb *soler* plus the infinitive. *Soler* cannot be translated into any word in English.

soler

	Singular	Plural
1	solía	solíamos
2	solías	solíais
3	solía	solían

Fig. 5.10

Examples:

1. *Yo solía ir al cine todos los días.*

2. *Solíamos ir a pie para la escuela cuando éramos jóvenes.*

Indirect Speech/Direct Speech

The imperfect is also used for indirect or reported speech. Direct speech is when a speaker is repeating what someone else said verbatim. Indirect speech is when a speaker says what someone else said that is not verbatim. Look at the following sentences.

> *My sister said, "I am going to Spain."* (direct speech)
> *My sister said that she was going to Spain.* (indirect/reported speech)

> *Mi hermana me dijo, "Voy para España."* (direct speech)
> *Mi hermana me dijo que iba para España.* (indirect/reported speech)

Problematic Verbs

There are a few verbs that students have trouble with when it comes to using either the imperfect or the preterit. These verbs are *ser, estar, querer, poder, creer,* and *tener.* Instead of finding the answer in grammar books, I decided to ask native speakers what they thought. These are their answers, which may or may not be correct:

ser

"La película era/fue larga."

I asked my friend Guillermo what the differences between these two sentences were, and he said, "Whoa! They're the same!"

He and many of my other Mexican friends agree that they are the same. However, two Mexican speakers told me that they would say the first sentence if they were describing the movie. They would say the second one if they had just finished watching the movie.

"La Guerra de Secesión era/fue un desastre."

Although both can be used here, *fue* is more common and makes more sense. I was told that saying *era* wouldn't impede the overall meaning. I would say that *fue* is required because the Civil War is a historical event.

"Cuando yo era/fui niño, yo…"

Although Spanish speakers can't explain why, they know that saying *fui* is incorrect. You have to use *era* because it is narrative background.

"Mi padre era/fue medico."

Saying *era* in this sentences means that the father was a doctor during his life and died. Saying *fue* means that the father was a doctor at one point in his life, but he either retired or changed professions.

"El libro era/fue escrito por Cervantes."

Here *fue* is required because it is a passive voice construction.

tener

"Mi hermano me dijo que tenía/tuvo un libro de francés."

My friend translated these two sentences for me in English, and his translations surprised me. The imperfect sentence translates as *My brother told me that he had a book.* The second is. *My brother told me that he used to have a book.* I was surprised because I had always learned that the habitual past in English (used to + verb) translates to the imperfect in Spanish. But in this sentence the preterit is translated as "used to + verb." The only reason I can think of for this translation is the fact that the action of having something can't be repeated over and over. And it can also be explained by applying the concept of aspect. The preterit implies perfective aspect (or complete), and the imperfect implies imperfective aspect (or incomplete).

"Yo tenía/tuve frío."

"Yo tenía frío" means "I was cold." And "Yo tuve frío" means "I got cold." The imperfect sentence is a description. The preterit sentence is a sudden occurrence. This works for other expressions that require *tener* + adjective.

"Yo tuve una carta."

According to many books, the preterit of *tener* means *received.* But my Spanish speaking friends don't agree with that. The above sentence means "I used to have a letter." Guillermo told he would've said *Yo recibí una carta* if he wanted to say *I received a letter.*

querer

"Yo me quería/quise ir."

According to my Mexican friends, these two sentences are the same. But they would prefer to say *quería.* A Spaniard told me that they are not the same. He would use the preterit if he wanted to do it at that moment. Many books say that the preterit of *querer* means *tried.* But most Spanish speakers disagree with this. For them it is easier to use *tratar.* Ybette told me that the imperfect sentence means *I wanted to go (but maybe I didn't)*. The preterit sentence means *I wanted to go and I did*.

When *querer* is used in the preterit and negated, it means *refused*. For example:

"No me quise ir." – *"I refused to go."*

"Cuando la chica vio el caballo, lo quería/quiso de inmediato."

In this case only the preterit is possible. This is because the action of wanting wasn't continuous; it was a reaction to another action.

estar

"Yo estaba/estuve aquí a las nueve."

Many grammar books say that the imperfect sentence means *I was here at nine* whereas the preterit sentence means *I arrived here at nine*. I asked some Spanish speakers about this, and they told me that the second sentence stretches the meaning of *estar*. If they wanted to say "arrived," they would say *Yo llegué aquí a las nueve*. Ybette told me that the imperfect sentence means *I was here at nine* whereas the preterit sentence emphasizes the fact that the person was there at nine: *I WAS here at nine*.

"El hombre estaba/estuvo borracho."

Saying *El hombre estaba borracho* is simply a description. To say *El hombre estuvo borracho* you have to also indicate a place where he was drunk. For example: *El hombre estuvo borracho en el restaurante*. This also works with other adjectives.

Examples:
La chica estaba contenta.
La chica estuvo contenta en la fiesta.

creer

"La chica dijo que creía/creyó en Papá Noel."

The imperfect sentence is an example of indirect speech. You could also say *La chica dijo, 'Yo creo en Papá Noel.'* The preterit sentence translates into *The girl said she used to believe in Santa Claus*. This is another example of a preterit verb that means "used to." The act of believing isn't an action that can be repeated over and over again.

poder

"El estudiante podía/pudo hacer su tarea."

The imperfect sentence indicates that the student had the ability to do his homework. The preterit sentence indicates that the student had the ability to do his homework and succeeded; his homework is finished.

"El estudiante no podía/pudo hacer su tarea."

The imperfect sentence indicates that the student was capable of doing his homework, but for some reason he didn't do it. The preterit sentence indicates that the student was not capable of doing his homework; he tried and failed.

"Used to" in the Sense of "Would"

English often uses the modal verb *would* where an imperfect verb would be used in Spanish. Look at the following sentence.

I would watch TV all day when I was young.
Yo miraba la television todo el día cuando era joven.

If the modal verb *would* is conveying a hypothetical situation, the conditional is used. But when it is used in a sentence like the one above, the imperfect is used.

These two past tenses require a lot of practice to understand correctly. The rules in this chapter should clarify when to use one or the other.

Chapter 6
Demystifying the Spanish Subjunctive I

The Spanish subjunctive is probably the most difficult thing that you will ever encounter in Spanish grammar. The subjunctive frustrates many students. It's easy to see why. It has so many uses and takes up nearly forty pages in Benjamin & Butt's book *A New Reference Grammar of Modern Spanish*. I will explain the subjunctive the traditional way and my way. One thing that many students assume about the subjunctive is that it always conveys doubt. This is only one of the many uses.

Conjugating the subjunctive is relatively easy. Take the *yo* form of the present indicative, remove the *o*, and add the appropriate endings. It is said that the verbs take "opposite" endings.

	sing. (-ar)	plural	sing. (-er)	plural	sing. (-ir)	plural
1	hable	hablemos	coma	comamos	viva	vivamos
2	hables	habléis	comas	comáis	vivas	viváis
3	hable	hablen	coma	coman	viva	vivan

Fig. 6.1

There are six commonly used verbs that are irregular in the present subjunctive. You can remember them with the acronym DISHES.

Dar
Ir
Ser
Haber
Estar
Saber

	ser sing.	plural	estar sing.	plural	haber sing.	plural
1	sea	seamos	esté	estemos	haya	hayamos
2	seas	seáis	estés	estéis	hayas	hayáis
3	sea	sean	esté	estén	haya	hayan

Fig. 6.2

	dar sing.	plural	ir sing.	plural	saber sing.	plural
1	dé	demos	vaya	vayamos	sepa	sepamos
2	des	deis	vayas	vayáis	sepas	sepáis
3	dé	den	vaya	vayan	sepa	sepan

Fig. 6.3

*Some teachers prefer not to teach *dar* and *haber* when they begin to teach which verbs are irregular in the present subjunctive. If we remove these two verbs, we can use the following acronym: SEIS.

Ser
Estar
Ir
Saber

The traditional method of teaching the subjunctive is to explain its uses in nominal clauses, adjective clauses, and adverbial clauses. These clauses are always dependent; therefore, there must also be an independent/main clause. In nominal and adjective clauses there must also be a change of subject from the independent clause to the independent clause.

Nominal clause- when the clause is the direct object of the verb of the main clause.
Example:
Quiero que vengas conmigo.
The direct object of *querer* is "que vengas conmigo." It is the nominal clause. There is also a change of subject from the independent clause to the dependent clause.

Adjective clause- when the clause modifies the direct object of the verb in the main clause.

Example:
Busco alguien que hable francés.
The direct object *alguien* is being modified by the adjective clause *que hable francés.*

Adverbial clause- when the clause modifies the verb of the main clause.

Example:
Puedes jugar cuando termines tu tarea.
The adverbial clause is *cuando termines tu tarea.*

All this may sound like Greek to you, but don't worry. Other students feel the same way. I explain the subjunctive with the acronym DINNER. But this only applies to nominal and adjective clauses.

Doubt/uncertainty
Influence
Non-existence
Negating certain verbs
Emotional reactions
Required conjunctions

Examples of subjunctive

1. Dudo que venga. – I doubt he is coming.
2. No estamos seguros de que tengas razón.- We're not sure that you're right.
3. Ella quiere que yo me vaya. – She wants me to go away.
4. Mi madre me dice que limpie mi cuarto. – My mother tells me to clean my room.
5. Me alegro de que estés aquí. – I'm glad you're here.

6. Ellos temen que esté muerto su padre. – They fear that their father is dead.
7. Siempre estudio a menos de que mi novia esté conmigo. – I always study unless my girlfriend is with me.
8. Mis padres trabajan para que tengamos dinero. – My parents work so that we will have money.

Doubt/Uncertainty

The subjunctive is used with verbs of doubt or uncertainty. It is a common misconception that the subjunctive always conveys a sense of doubt, but this is not the case. It has other uses as well. Some verbs of doubt include, but are not limited to, *dudar, no estar seguro,* and *no estar cierto.*

Choose the correct form of the verb.
1. El profesor duda que sus estudiantes (hacen/hagan) su tarea.
2. No dudamos que (hay/haya) un problema.
3. No estoy seguro de que (comprendo/comprenda).
4. Es cierto que la escuela (necesita/necesite) más dinero.
5. Es posible que (llueve/llueva).

Influence

The subjunctive is used when a verb in the main clause is influencing the subject in the dependent clause.

Choose the correct form of the verb.
1. Yo quiero que tú (aprendes/aprendas) español.
2. Mi madre me dice que (limpio/limpie) mi cuarto.
3. El profesor hace que sus estudiantes (van/vayan) a clase.
4. Mi hermano desea que su perro no (duerme/duerma) en su cama.
5. Los profesores exigen que sus estudiantes (vienen/vengan) a clase.

Non-existence

The subjunctive is used when something isn't known to exist.

Examples
1. Buscamos un secretario que hable inglés. – We're looking for a secretary who speaks English. (We don't know if such a secretary exists.)
2. Tenemos un secretario que habla inglés. – We have a secretary who speaks English. (We know that such a secretary exists.)
3. ¿Tiene usted un secretario que sepa inglés? – Do you have a secretary who knows English? (We don't know if such a secretary exists.)
4. Usted tiene un secretario que sabe inglés. – You have a secretary who knows English. (We know that such a secretary exists.)
5. No hay nadie aquí que sepa inglés. – There is nobody here who knows English. (We know that such a person DOES NOT exist.)
6. Buscamos una casa donde podamos criar a nuestros niños. - We're looking for a house where we can raise our children. (We don't know if such a house exists.)

Choose the correct form of the verb.
1. Necesito un estudiante que (tiene/tenga) facilidad con las computadoras.
2. ¿Hay un profesor aquí que (sabe/sepa) italiano?
3. Tenemos dos estudiantes que (son/sean) buenos con las computadoras.
4. No hay ningún profesor que (habla/hable) español.
5. La estudiante busca un tutor que (puede/pueda) ayudarla con su español.

Negating certain verbs

The subjunctive is used when certain verbs are negated. The most common ones are *pensar* and *creer.* The subjunctive is also used when the following verbs are negated: *parecer, suponer, sospechar,* and *esperar.*

According to Butt & Benjamin, when *esperar* is used in an affirmative form, the mood of the dependent verb changes its meaning. If the dependent verb is indicative, *esperar* means *to expect.* When the dependent verb is subjunctive, *esperar* means *to hope.* Whenever *esperar* is negated, the subjunctive is required (259).

Examples:
1. No creo que tengas razón - I don't think that you're right.
2. No pensamos que sea una buena idea. - We don't think that it's a good idea.

Emotional Reactions

The subjunctive is used when describing an emotional reaction to something else.

Examples:
1. Me alegro de que venga mi hermana. – I'm glad my sister is coming.
2. Tememos que el perro esté muerto. – We fear that the dog is dead.

Choose the correct form of the verb.
1. Tenemos miedo de que el coche no (funciona/funcione).
2. Estoy contento que me (vienes/vengas) a mí.
3. Ella está triste que su hijo (está/esté) enfermo.
4. La profesora está sorprendida que sus estudiantes (aprenden/aprendan) tanto.
5. La niña está celosa que su hermana mayor (tiene/tenga) caramelos.

Required Conjunctions

Certain conjunctions always require the subjunctive. These are often called interdependent conjunctions. You can remember them with the acronym A-SPACE.

A menos de que - unless
Sino que – but rather that
Para que - so that
Antes de que - before
Con tal que – provided that
En caso de que - in case that

Examples:
1. Vamos a estudiar a menos de que nuestros amigos vengan. – We're going to study unless our friends come.
2. El profesor explica el subjuntivo para que sus estudiantes lo comprendan. – The professor explains the subjunctive so that his students understand it.

When There Is No Change In Subject

When there is no change in subject from the independent verb to the dependent verb, neither the subjunctive nor the indicative is used. Instead, the infinitive is used.

Examples:

Yo quiero ir al cine. – I want to go to the movies.
Creo necesitar estudiar más. – I think that I need to study more.
Note: "Creo que necesito estudiar más." is not correct. (It is used colloquially.)

Impersonal Expressions

The subjunctive is required after certain impersonal expressions. Even though most of these expressions fall under a category in the DINNER acronym, it is helpful to have a list of them to look up easily and conveniently.

No es cierto que_____	It not certain that_____
No es seguro que_____	It is unsure that_____
(No) es possible que_____	It is (im)possible that
(No) es probable que_____	It is (im)probable that_____
Es dudoso que_____	It is doubtful that_____

Adverbial Clauses

The subjunctive is used in adverbial clauses where the verb after the conjunction conveys a future action. The most commonly used conjunctions are *cuando, hasta que*, and *después de que*. However, if the verb after these conjunctions does not convey a future action and conveys a habitual action, the present indicative is used. It is also impossible to use the future or the conditional after these conjunctions unless you are asking a question.

Examples:

1. *Voy a leer hasta que los niños se duerman.* (The subjunctive is used because the verb in the dependent clause conveys a future action.)
2. *Leo hasta que los niños se duermen.* (The indicative is used because the verb does not convey a future action. It conveys a present, habitual action.)

Choose the correct form of the verb.

1. La profesora nos dará los exámenes cuando están/estén listos.
2. La profesora nos da los exámenes cuando están/estén listos.
3. Sabrás utilizar la computadora después de que lees/leas el manual.
4. Los empleados aquí siempre trabajan hasta que están/estén cansados.
5. ¿Cuándo vengas/vendrás conmigo para España?

Other Adverbial Clauses

Adverbs are words that modify verbs. There are three types: adverbs of time, manner, and place. This also applies to adverbial clauses. The above examples are examples of adverbial clauses of time.

Time
cuando
hasta que
después de que

Manner
aunque
como
de manera que
de modo que

Place
donde

When you use an adverbial clause of time, you have to ask yourself if the action is going to occur in the future. When you use an adverbial clause of manner or place, you have to ask yourself if the situation is known or unknown. Look at the following examples.

No somos tan tontos como crees.
We're not as dumb as you think.

No somos tan tontos como creas.
We're not as dumb as you may think.

In the first sentence speaker A *knows* that speaker B thinks that he is dumb. In the second sentence speaker A does *not* know how dumb speaker B thinks he is.

More examples:

Voy a hacer el curso aunque es difícil.
I'm going to take the class even though it is difficult.

Voy a hacer el curso aunque sea difícil.
I'm going to take the class even though it may be difficult.

In the first sentence the speaker knows that the class is difficult. In the second sentence the speaker does not whether or not the class will be difficult.

More Examples :

Les hablaré de manera que me entienden.
I will speak to them in such a way that they will understand me.

Les hablaré de manera que me entiendan.
I will speak to them in such a way that they may understand me.

More Examples:

Vamos a ir adonde quieres.
We'll go where you want.

Vamos a ir adonde quieras.
We'll go where you (may) want.

Don't confuse this use of *donde* with its use in adjective clauses (non-existence). In the previous sentences *donde* is modifying a verb, not a noun.

Trick Question

Is the indicative or the subjunctive used in the following sentence?

Juan no está seguro de cómo (aprobó/aprobara) su examen de conducir.
Juan isn't sure how he passed his driving test.

You probably chose the subjunctive because this sentence deals with doubt or uncertainty. But this sentence does not contain a nominal clause. Doubt/uncertainty only applies to nominal clauses. This sentence does, however, contain an adverbial clause. In adverbial clauses, the subjunctive is used when the situation is not known to the speaker. Juan has already passed his driving test, but he does not how he passed it. In the following sentence the subjunctive is required because it contains a nominal clause that expresses doubt.

Juan no está seguro de que haya aprobado su examen de conducir.
Juan isn't sure that he has passed his driving test.

This sentence indicates that Juan has taken his test, but he does not yet know whether or not he passed it.

As you can see, the subjunctive is easy to form but hard to learn how to use. It requires a lot of time and practice to master. This chapter deals with the present subjunctive. The next chapter deals with the imperfect subjunctive and other uses of the subjunctive in Spanish.

Don't continue with the subjunctive in chapter 7 until you've learned all the uses of the subjunctive in this chapter.

Chapter 7
Demystifying the Spanish Subjunctive II

You learned the present subjunctive in chapter 6. Now, you will learn the other subjunctive tenses. The rules still apply to these forms of the subjunctive.

Imperfect Subjunctive

The imperfect subjunctive is used for the same reasons as the present subjunctive, but the verb in the main clause is in a past tense (usually the imperfect or the preterit tense).

The imperfect subjunctive is formed by taking the 3rd person plural form of the verb, removing the ending *ron*, and adding the appropriate endings.

hablar
hablaron

	sing.	**plural**
1	habla*ra*	hablá*ramos*
2	habla*ras*	habla*rais*
3	habla*ra*	habla*ran*

Fig. 7.1

These are called the *ra* endings. There is another set of endings called the *se* endings. They mean the same thing, but the *ra* forms are used more in conversation. The *se* endings are reserved for writing in most Spanish speaking countries. The *se* endings are commonly used in conversation in Spain.

	sing.	**plural**
1	habla*se*	hablá*semos*
2	habla*ses*	habla*seis*
3	habla*se*	habla*sen*

Fig. 7.2

Examples of Imperfect Subjunctive

1. Mi madre quería que yo limpiara mi cuarto. – My mother wanted me to clean my room.
2. No estábamos seguros de que vinieras. – We weren't sure that you were coming.
3. Tenía miedo de que mi perro estuviera muerto. – I was afraid that my dog was dead.
4. El profesor les dijo a sus estudiantes que hicieran su tarea. – The professor told his students to do their homework.
5. Ella quería ir al cine antes de que lloviera. – She wanted to go to the movies before it rained.
6. La estudiante le llamó a un tutor para que comprendiera mejor el subjuntivo. – The student called a tutor so that she might understand the subjunctive better.

Choose the correct form of the verb.

1. Mi padre quería que yo (corté/cortara) el césped.
2. No estaba seguro de que ella (sabía/supiera) la respuesta correcta.
3. Ella estaba segura de que (sabíamos/supiéramos) la verdad.
4. No había nadie que (hablaba/hablara) inglés.
5. ¿Había alguien que (sabía/supiera) inglés?

Note for Literature Students

When you read Old Spanish literature, you will see the imperfect *ra* verb forms used in a different way. The *ra* forms of the imperfect subjunctive used to be used as the past perfect indicative forms; it didn't require the verb *haber*. After its use as the past perfect indicative faded away, it became the conditional. That's why expressions like *Yo quisiera* ____ still exist as meaning *I'd like* ____ . (In this case you can't say *Yo quisiese* ____ .). After being used as the conditional, it became the new imperfect subjunctive form. The *se* endings were actually the only imperfect endings which is why the *se* endings are used in Old Spanish literature and in many formal contexts today.

When There Is No Change In Subject

The past infinitve is used when the action of the second verb occurs before the action of the independent verb.
No creo que hayas estudiado lo suficiente. - I don't think you've studied enough.
No creo haber estudiado lo suficiente. - I don't think I've studied enough.

Imperfect Subjunctive in Adverbial Clauses

The imperfect subjunctive can also be used in adverbial clauses just like the present subjunctive. In adverbial clauses of manner and place, it's still a matter of whether something is known to be true or not. But in adverbial clauses of time, it's a little different.
The present subjunctive is used after conjunctions like *cuando* and *hasta que* when the verb refers to future action. The imperfect subjunctive is used after these conjunctions when the action of the verb refers to a future action in relation the first verb.

Example:
Voy a leer hasta que los niños se duerman.
I'm going to read until the kids fall asleep.
(present subjunctive: action occurs in the future)

Leo hasta que los niños se duermen.
I read until the kids fall asleep.
(present indicative: present habitual action)

Iba a leer hasta que los niños se durmieran.
I was going to read until the kids fell asleep.
(imperfect subjunctive: action occurs in the future in relation to the verb *leer*)

Leía hasta que los niños se dormían.
I used to read until the kids fell asleep.
(imperfect indicative: past habitual action)

Present Perfect Subjunctive

The present perfect subjunctive is used when the verb in the main clause is in the present indicative, but the action of the verb in the dependent clause occurs before the action of the main verb.

It is formed by taking the present subjunctive of the verb *haber* and adding the past participle of the verb.

Example:
Dudo que hayas hecho tu tarea.
I doubt that you have done your homework.

Dudar is in the present indicative, but the action of the verb *hacer* occurs before the action of the verb *dudar*. Look at the following sentence.

Dudo que hagas tu tarea.
I doubt that you are doing your homework.

Dudar is in the present indicative, and the action of *hacer* occurs at the same moment. Therefore, the present subjunctive is used.

haber (present subjunctive)

	Singular	Plural
1	haya	hayamos
2	hayas	hayáis
3	haya	hayan

Fig. 7.3

Past Perfect Subjunctive

The past perfect subjunctive is used when the verb in the main clause is in a past tense, but the action of the verb in the dependent clause occurs before the action of the main verb.

It is formed by taking the imperfect subjunctive of the verb *haber* and adding the past participle of the verb.

Example

Dudé que hubiera hecho su tarea.
I doubted that he had done his homework.

Dudar is in the preterit tense, and the verb *hacer* is in the past perfect subjunctive because the action occurs before the action of the verb *dudar*.

Dudé que hiciera su tarea.
I doubted that he was doing his homework.

The actions of the verbs *dudar* and *hacer* are simultaneous.

Conditional Sentences

The past subjunctive and past perfect subjunctive are used in conditional sentences. There are three main types of conditional sentences in Spanish.

	"Si" clause	"Result" clause
1	Present Indicative	Simple Future
2	Imperfect Subjunctive	Simple Conditional
3	Past Perfect Subjunctive	Simple Conditional Perfect

Fig. 7.4

The *si* clause (*if* clause in English) conveys a hypothetical situation. The result clause conveys what would be the case if the *si* clause were true.

Examples:
1. Si haces tu tarea, aprenderás más. - If you do your homework, you will learn more.
2. Si tuviera más dinero, iría a España. - If I had more money, I would go to Spain.
3. Si hubiera tenido más dinero, habría ido a España. - If I had had more money, I would've gone to Spain.

Sequence of Tenses/Moods

Independent Verb	Dependent Verb
present indicative	1. present subjunctive
	2. present perfect subjunctive
imperfect/preterit	1. imperfect subjunctive
	2. past perfect subjunctive
future	present subjunctive
future perfect	present subjunctive
conditional	imperfect subjunctive
conditional perfect	past perfect subjunctive
imperative	present subjunctive

Fig. 7.5

The first column shows the independent verb. The second column shows what form of the subjunctive goes with the verb form in the first column. Although there are more possibilities, these are the most common. If the first verb is present indicative, there are two possibilities. The verb in the dependent clause is present subjunctive if the action of the verb is simultaneous with the action of the independent verb or if the action of the verb is a future action. There are also two choices if the independent verb is imperfect or preterit. The imperfect subjunctive is used if the action of the dependent verb is simultaneous with the action of the independent verb. If the action of the dependent verb occurred before the action of the independent verb, the past perfect subjunctive is used.

Using the Subjunctive with ojalá

Ojalá	Verb in 2nd Clause
Ojalá + present subjunctive	I hope + present/future
Ojalá + present perfect subjunctive	I hope + present perfect
Ojalá + imperfect subjunctive	I wish + past
Ojalá + past perfect subjunctive	I wish + past perfect

Fig. 7.6

Examples
Ojalá que ella venga.
I hope she comes.

Ojalá que haya venido.
I hope she has come.

Ojalá que ella viniera.
I wish she came. / I wish she would come. (This is not actually correct English)

Ojalá que ella hubiera venido.
I wish she had come.

Using the Subjunctive with como si

It is mandatory to use either the imperfect or the past perfect subjunctive after *como si*.

Verb in the 1st clause	Verb in the 2nd clause
present indicative	imperfect subjunctive
imperfect/preterit	past perfect subjunctive
future	imperfect subjunctive
conditional	imperfect subjunctive

Fig. 7.7

Examples

1. Habla español como si fuera nativo.
2. Contaba la historia como si hubiera estado allí.
3. Le explicaré todo esto como si él no supiera nada.

Commands

hablar

	Singular	Plural
1	---------	hablemos
2	hables	habléis
3	hable	hablen

Fig. 7.8

The command forms for the pronouns *tú* and *vosotros* have special affirmative forms. For the *tú* form, remove the -s from the *tú* form of the present indicative.

Hablas - Habla

For the the *vosotros* form, remove the -r from the infinitive and add -d.

Hablar - Hablad

All other forms use the present subjunctive. All negative commands require the present subjunctive. There is no command for the *yo* form.

The following sentences are affirmative. Make them negative.

1. Come la manzana.

2. Hablad en inglés.

3. Vayamos al cine.

Set Phrases

There are some set phrases in Spanish that use the subjunctive. The following are probably the most common three.

sea lo que sea - whatever it may be
venga lo que venga - come what may
o sea que - in other words

Future Subjunctive

The future subjunctive is obsolete in modern Spanish but is still in Old Spanish literature and sometimes legal documents today. It's relatively easy to conjugate.

hablar

	sing.	**plural**
1	habla*re*	hablá*remos*
2	habla*res*	habla*reis*
3	habla*re*	habla*ren*

Fig. 7.9

As you can see, it is very similar to the imperfect subjunctive. Take the imperfect subjunctive (-ra forms) and replace the -a with an -e.

It is good to know this in case you see when you are reading, but don't try to use it if you don't have to. One of my friends from Mexico knew what this was, but he also told me that many uneducated Mexicans use the future subjunctive forms when they want to use the imperfect subjunctive.

When the future subjunctive is used in legal documents, it usually translates into "he/she who ____."

"El/ella que tuviere la mayoría de votos será presidente."
"He/she who has to most votes will be the president."

Future Perfect Subjunctive

You may never see this form of the subjunctive. It is formed by taking the future subjunctive of the verb *haber* and adding the past participle.

haber

	sing.	plural
1	hubiere	hubiéremos
2	hubieres	hubiereis
3	hubiere	hubieren

Fig. 7.10

Example

"La persona que hubiere ganado la elección será presidente."
"The person who has won the election will be president."

Brandon Simpson

Chapter 8
Conclusion

By now, you should have a clear understanding of written accents in Spanish, the differences between *ser* and *estar*, the differences between *por* and *para*, the distinction between the imperfect and the preterit, and the subjunctive mood.

The primary function of the written accent is to show where the stress is on a Spanish word that breaks a common stress pattern. However, the written accent has other functions that are explained in chapter 2.

The difference between *ser* and *estar* used to be explained that *ser* expresses permanence and that *estar* is temporary. In chapter 3 *ser/estar* is explained with other methods. The *permanent/temporary* explanation is flawed.

Por and *para* are two very tricky Spanish prepositions. They usually translate to *for* in English, but they are not interchangeable. They are explained in chapter 4.

The imperfect and the preterit are also tricky, but they are not as hard to learn as some think. They only require practice. They are explained in chapter 5.

The Spanish subjunctive is explained in chapters 6 and 7. The subjunctive is very difficult. In fact, it would require a book of its own if it were explained fully and in absolute great detail. However, I attempted to explain it as well as possible in this book.

If there are any other troublesome grammatical concepts that are not explained in this book, check out Appendix D for a list of recommended books. Or if you need to review English grammar in order to better understand Spanish grammar, consult books on English grammar.

Answers to Exercises

Chapter 2

(The answers are italicized.)

1. ¿Que/*qué* hora es?

2. Tiene algo para mi/*mí*.

3. Necesito el/*él* libro.

4. Mi hermano no quiere este/*éste* carro.

5. ¿De donde/*dónde* eres?

6. ¿Cual/*cuál* es la capital de México?

7. Uno debería aprender una lengua como/*cómo* la aprenden los niños.

8. ¿Como/*cómo* te llamas?

9. ¿Cuantos/*cuántos* años tienes?

10. ¿Quien/*quién* es usted?

Exercise 2

Me llamo Marcos de la Vega. Soy de España. Tengo dieciséis años. Este semestre estudio la literatura española, inglés, francés, matemáticas, geología y biología. Me interesan muchos las lenguas extranjeras. Cuando vaya a la universidad, me gustaría estudiar la lingüística. La lingüística será fácil para mi puesto que soy multilingüe.

Tengo dos hermanos. Viven en México. Mi hermano Juan

tiene veintidós años y tiene un niño. Él tiene dos años. A su mujer y él les gustaría tener más niños en el futuro. Mi otro hermano Miguel tiene veinte años y vive en el Perú. Ambos mis hermanos son bilingües. Hablan español e inglés.

Chapter 3

1. ¿Qué hora *es*/está?
2. Soy/*estoy* enfermo.
3. Mi hermano *es*/está estudiante.
4. Mis primos *son*/están de Inglaterra.
5. La fiesta *es*/está en la casa de Juan.
6. George Bush *es*/está republicano.
7. ¿Dónde es/*está* tu carro?
8. Mi hermanito *es*/estás muy bajo.
9. La temperatura es/*está* muy baja hoy.
10. ¿De dónde *eres*/está?
11. Ese hombre *es*/está muy gordo.
12. Aquellas chicas *son*/están muy flacas, ¿no?

1. Yo estoy muy cansado.
2. La profesora es muy inteligente.
3. Nosotros somos de México.
4. Son las dos de la tarde.
5. Arnold Schwarzenegger es el gobernador de California.
6. Mi padre está enojado conmigo.
7. ¿Qué hora es?
8. La reunión es aquí en dos horas.
9. París está en Francia.
10. ¿Cómo eres/estás tú?
   The meaning changes from *What are you like?* to *How are you?*
11. Ese hombre es/está borracho.
   Ser borracho means to be an alcoholic. *Estar borracho* means to be drunk.

12. La nieve es blanca.

1. I am drunk.
   Yo estoy borracho/a.
2. That man is an alcoholic.
   Ese hombre es borracho.
3. This price is really high.
   Este precio es muy alto.
4. My son is tall.
   Mi hijo es alto.
5. It is 3 o'clock.
   Son las tres.
6. My mom is a teacher.
   Mi madre es profesora.
7. Our dog is small.
   Nuestro perro es pequeño.
8. Where is the meeting?
   ¿Dónde es la reunión?
9. His friend is Mexican.
   Su amigo/a es mexicano/a.
10. Her friend is from Spain.
    Su amigo/a es de España.
11. San Juan is in Puerto Rico.
    San Juan está en Puerto Rico.
12. My girlfriend is very happy.
    Mi novia está contenta.

Chapter 4

1. Estudio mucho *para* conseguir una buena nota.
2. Anduvimos *para/por* la calle.
   Anduvimos para la calle. – We walked to (towards) the street.
   Anduvimos por la calle. – We walked through the street.
3. Cuatro *por* cuatro son dieciséis.
4. Viajamos *para/por* España.

Viajamos para España. – We traveled to (towards) Spain.
Viajamos por España. – We traveled through Spain.
5. El libro fue escrito *por* Nebrija.
6. Los estudiantes estudiaron *por* dos horas.
7. Me gustaría un café, *por* favor.
8. Noventa *por* ciento de la clase entiende la lección.
9. Aprendo francés *para* que mis clientes francófonos me comprendan.
10. Aprendo francés *por*que mis clientes francófonos no hablan mucho inglés.
11. La tarea es *para* las dos de la tarde el 2 de mayo.
12. Este regalo es *para* mi hijo.
13. Tengo que estudiar *para* el examen.
14. *Por* casualidad, ¿sabes la hora?
15. Voy a trabajar *para/por* Señor Jaime.
    Voy a trabajar para Señor Jaime. – I'm going to work for Mister Jaime. (Mr. Jaime is my boss.)
    Voy a trabajar por Señor Jaime. – I'm going to work in Mr. Jaime's place.
16. ¿*Por* quién votaste?
17. ¿Cuál es más fácil *para* ti?
18. *Para* un japonés, habla inglés muy bien.

1. My son studies Spanish because he wants to improve his CV.
    Mi hijo estudia español porque quiere mejorar su CV.
2. Class was canceled because of the weather.
    La clase fue cancelada por el tiempo.
3. We went to Spain.
    Fuimos para España.
4. We traveled through Spain.
    Viajamos por España.
5. I need to study for the exam.
    Necesito estudiar para el examen.
6. The girl watched TV for three hours.
    La chica miró la televisión por tres horas.
7. Three times three is nine.

Tres por tres son nueve.
8. Five is fifty per cent of ten.
   Cinco son cincuenta por ciento de diez.
9. The homework is due on Friday.
   La tarea es para el viernes.
10. I have something for you.
    Tengo algo para ti/usted/ustedes/vosotros.

Chapter 5

1. It was raining. (imperfect)
   Llovía.
2. I saw my teacher. (preterit)
   Vi a mi profesor.
3. I was reading a book when I saw a cat. (imperfect, preterit)
   Leía un libro cuando vi un gato.
4. She read this book three times. (preterit)
   Ella leyó este libro tres veces.
5. They didn't come because they were tired. (preterit, imperfect)
   Ellos no vinieron porque estaban cansados.
6. We used to go to the movies all the time. (imperfect)
   Íbamos al cine todo el tiempo,
7. What were you doing? (imperfect)
   ¿Qué hacías?
8. What did you do? (preterit)
   ¿Qué hiciste?
9. It rained for three hours. (preterit)
   Llovió por tres horas.
10. The house was small and white. (imperfect)
    La casa era pequeña y blanca.
11. I ate there everyday. (imperfect)
    Comía allí todos los días.
12. What did you eat? (preterit)
    ¿Qué comiste?
13. What were you eating? (imperfect)
    ¿Qué comías?

14. The man was singing in French. (imperfect)
El hombre cantaba en francés.
15. The man sang in French. (preterit)
El hombre canto en francés.

Chapter 6

Doubt/uncertainty

1. El profesor duda que sus estudiantes (hacen/*hagan*) su tarea.
2. No dudamos que (*hay*/haya) un problema.
3. No estoy seguro de que (comprendo/*comprenda*).
4. Es cierto que la escuela (*necesita*/necesite) más dinero.
5. Es posible que (llueve/*llueva*).

Influence

1. Yo quiero que tú (aprendes/*aprendas*) español.
2. Mi madre me dice que yo (limpio/*limpie*) mi cuarto.
3. El profesor hace que sus estudiantes (van/*vayan*) en clase.
4. Mi hermano desea que su perro no (duerme/*duerma*) en su cama.
5. Los profesores exigen (require) que sus estudiantes (vienen/*vengan*) en clase.

Non-existence

1. Necesito a un estudiante que (es/*sea*) bueno con las computadoras.
2. ¿Hay un profesor aquí que (sabe/*sepa*) italiano?
3. Tenemos dos estudiantes que (*son*/sean) buenos con las computadoras.
4. No hay ningún profesor que (habla/*hable*) español.
5. La estudiante busca a un tutor que (puede/*pueda*) ayudarla con su español

Emotional Reactions

1. Tenemos miedo de que el coche no (funciona/*funcione*).
2. Estoy contento que me (vienes/*vengas*) a mí.
3. Ella está triste que su hijo (está/*esté*) enfermo.
4. La profesora está sorprendida que sus estudiantes (aprenden/*aprendan*) tanto.
5. La niña está celosa que su hermana mayor (tiene/*tenga*) caramelos

Adverbial Clauses

1. La profesora nos dará los exámenes cuando están/*estén* listos.
2. La profesora nos da los exámenes cuando *están*/estén listos.
3. Sabrás utilizar la computadora después de que lees/*leas* el manual.
4. Los empleados aquí siempre trabajan hasta que *están*/estén cansados.
5. ¿Cuándo vengas/*vendrás* conmigo para España?

Chapter 7

Imperfect Subjunctive

1. Mi padre quería que yo (corté/*cortara*) el césped.
2. No estaba seguro que ella (sabía/*supiera*) la respuesta correcta.
3. Ella estaba segura que (*sabíamos*/supiéramos) la verdad.
4. No había nadie que (hablaba/*hablara*) inglés.
5. ¿Había alguien que (sabía/*supiera*) inglés?

Negative Commands

1. Come la manzana.
   No comas la manzana.
2. Hablad en inglés.
   No habléis en ingles.
3. Vayamos al cine.
   No vayamos al cine.

Appendix A:
Definitions of Grammatical Terms

This section is an abridged form of chapter two (pages 15-30) from my book *Learning Foreign Languages.* These are just definitions; there are no examples. For examples to these terms, consult *Learning Foreign Languages.*

Nouns & Adjectives

A noun is a person, place, or thing (tangible and intangible).

An adjective is a word that modifies a noun. They are usually descriptive words like big, red, small, etc.

Subject-Verb-Object

This is the typical word order in Spanish and English. A verb is an action word. The subject is who or what DOES the action of the verb. The direct object RECEiVES the action of the verb. The indirect object is usually the recipient of the direct object.

Predicate

The predicate is usually whatever comes after the verbs *to be, ser,* and *estar.*

Pronouns

Pronouns take the place of a noun.

Adverbs

Adverbs are words that modify the verb. There are three types: adverbs of manner, time, and place.

Conjunctions

Conjunctions are words that bring two separate sentences together.

Appendix B:
More on Spanish Nouns

Making Spanish nouns plural is very easy. There are four basic rules.

1. If the word ends in a vowel, add –s.
2. If the word ends in a consonant, add –es.
3. If the word ends in a –z, change the –z to a –c and add – es.
4. If the word is *llana* (2nd-to-last syllable is stressed) and ends in –s, there is no change.
   Ex. la crisis – las crisis (nothing changes)

Knowing the gender of Spanish nouns is very important. It is best to memorize the definite article with the noun, but there a few tricks that can tell what the gender is.

1. Most nouns that end in an –o are masculine.
   libro, muchacho
2. Most nouns that end in an –a are feminine.
   casa, muchacha
3. Nouns that end in –ión, -eza, -ez, or –dad are feminine.
   Navidad, civilización, estupidez, belleza
4. Nouns of Greek origin that end in –ta or –ma are masculine.
   planeta, programa, problema, cometa

Appendix C:
Figures Throughout this Book

Chapter 2

Monosyllabic Words that Require Accents

mi	my (possessive adj.)	mí	me (disjunctive pronoun)
el	the (def. art.)	él	he (pronoun)
de	from (preposition)	dé	form of *dar*
se	reflexive pronoun	sé	form of *saber*
si	if (conjunction)	sí	"yes"
mas	but (archaic form)	más	"more"

Fig. 2.1

Possible Diphthongs in Spanish

ai- habláis	ia- hiato
ei- veinte	ie- hierro
oi- sois	io- criollo
ui- fui	iu-ciudad
au- jaula	ua-actuar
eu-deuda	ue-fue
ou- NA	uo-antiguo

Fig. 2.2

Interrogatives/Conjunctions

¿qué?	what?	que	that
¿dónde?	where?	donde	where
¿cuándo?	when?	cuando	when
¿cómo?	how?	como	like, as
¿quién?	who?	quien	who
¿cuánto(a)(s)?	how much/many?	cuanto(a)(s)	how much/many

Fig. 2.3

Demonstrative Adjectives

this/these

	Singular	Plural
Masc.	este	estos
Fem.	esta	estas

Fig. 2.4

that/those

	Singular	Plural
Masc.	ese	esos
Fem.	esa	esas

Fig. 2.5

that/ those over there

	Singular	Plural
Masc.	aquel	aquellos
Fem.	aquella	aquellas

Fig. 2.6

Demonstrative Pronouns

this/these one(s)

	Singular	Plural
Masc.	éste	éstos
Fem.	ésta	éstas

Fig. 2.7

that/those one(s)

	Singular	Plural
Masc.	ése	ésos
Fem.	ésa	ésas

Fig. 2.8

that/ those one(s) over there

	Singular	Plural
Masc.	aquél	aquéllos
Fem.	aquélla	aquéllas

Fig. 2.9

Chapter 3

Conjugation of *ser* in the present tense

soy	somos
eres	sois
es	son

Fig. 3.1

Conjugation of *estar* in the present tense

estoy	estamos
estás	estáis
está	están

Fig. 3.2

Variable Adjectives

adjective	ser	estar
aburrido	boring	bored
bajo	short	low
alto	tall	high
borracho	alcoholic	drunk
enfermo	terminally ill	sick
muerto	stiff	dead
listo	bright (intelligent)	ready
seguro	secure/safe	sure

Fig. 3.3

91

-ar	-ando
-er	-iendo
-ir	-iendo

Fig. 3.4

Chapter 5

hablar (imperfect)

	Singular	Plural
1	habl*aba*	habl*ábamos*
2	habl*abas*	habl*abais*
3	habl*aba*	habl*aban*

Fig. 5.1

comer (imperfect)

	Singular	Plural
1	com*ía*	com*íamos*
2	com*ías*	com*íais*
3	com*ía*	com*ían*

Fig. 5.2

vivir (imperfect)

	Singular	Plural
1	viv*ía*	viv*íamos*
2	viv*ías*	viv*íais*
3	viv*ía*	viv*ían*

Fig. 5.3

ser (imperfect)

	Singular	Plural
1	era	éramos
2	eras	erais
3	era	eran

Fig. 5.4

ir (imperfect)

	Singular	Plural
1	iba	íbamos
2	ibas	ibais
3	iba	iban

Fig. 5.5

ver (imperfect)

	Singular	Plural
1	veía	veíamos
2	veías	veíais
3	veía	veían

Fig. 5.6

hablar (preterit)

	Singular	Plural
1	hablé	habl*amos*
2	habl*aste*	habl*asteis*
3	habl*ó*	habl*aron*

Fig. 5.7

comer (preterit)

	Singular	Plural
1	com*í*	com*imos*
2	com*iste*	com*isteis*
3	com*ió*	com*ieron*

Fig. 5.8

vivir (preterit)

	Singular	Plural
1	viv*í*	viv*imos*
2	viv*iste*	viv*isteis*
3	viv*ió*	viv*ieron*

Fig. 5.9

soler (imperfect)

	Singular	Plural
1	solía	solíamos
2	solías	solíais
3	solía	solían

Fig. 5.10

Chapter 6

Present Subjunctive

	-ar verbs		-er verbs		-ir verbs	
	sing.	**plural**	**sing.**	**plural**	**sing.**	**plural**
1	habl*e*	habl*emos*	com*a*	com*amos*	viv*a*	viv*amos*
2	habl*es*	habl*éis*	com*as*	com*áis*	viv*as*	viv*áis*
3	habl*e*	habl*én*	com*a*	com*an*	viv*a*	viv*an*

Fig. 6.1

Irregular Verbs in the Present Subjunctive

	ser		estar		haber	
	sing.	**plural**	**sing.**	**plural**	**sing.**	**plural**
1	sea	seamos	esté	estemos	haya	hayamos
2	seas	seáis	estés	estéis	hayas	hayáis
3	sea	sean	esté	estén	haya	hayan

Fig. 6.2

	dar		ir		saber	
	sing.	**plural**	**sing.**	**plural**	**sing.**	**plural**
1	dé	demos	vaya	vayamos	sepa	sepamos
2	des	déis	vayas	vayáis	sepas	sepáis
3	dé	den	vaya	vayan	sepa	sepan

Fig. 6.3

Chapter 7

hablar (imperfect subjunctive: -ra endings)

	sing.	plural
1	habla*ra*	hablá*ramos*
2	habla*ras*	habla*rais*
3	habla*ra*	habla*ran*

Fig. 7.1

hablar (imperfect subjunctive: -se endings)

	sing.	plural
1	habla*se*	hablá*semos*
2	habla*ses*	habla*seis*
3	habla*se*	habla*sen*

Fig. 7.2

haber (present subjunctive)

	Singular	Plural
1	haya	hayamos
2	hayas	hayáis
3	haya	hayan

Fig. 7.3

Conditional Sentences

	"Si" clause	"Result" clause
1	Present Indicative	Simple Future
2	Past Perfect Subjunctive	Simple Conditional
3	Past Perfect Subjunctive	Simple Conditional Perfect

Fig. 7.4

Concordance of Tenses/Moods (the most typical)

Independent Verb	Dependent Verb
present indicative	1. presente subjunctive 2. present perfect subjunctive
imperfect/preterit	1. imperfect subjunctive 2. past perfect subjunctive
future	present subjunctive
future perfect	present subjunctive
conditional	imperfect subjunctive
conditional perfect	past perfect subjunctive
imperative	present subjunctive

Fig. 7.5

Using the Subjunctive with ojalá

Ojalá	Verb in 2nd Clause
Ojalá + present subjunctive	I hope + present/future
Ojalá + present perfect subjunctive	I hope + present perfect
Ojalá + imperfect subjunctive	I wish + past
Ojalá + past perfect subjunctive	I wish + past perfect

Fig. 7.6

como si

Verb in the 1st clause	Verb in the 2nd clause
present indicative	imperfect subjunctive
imperfect/preterit	past perfect subjunctive
future	imperfect subjunctive
conditional	imperfect subjunctive

Fig. 7.7

Commands
hablar

	Singular	Plural
1	---------	hablemos
2	hables	habléis
3	hable	hablen

Fig. 7.8

hablar (future subjunctive)

	sing.	**plural**
1	habla*re*	hablá*remos*
2	habla*res*	habla*reis*
3	habla*re*	habla*ren*

Fig. 7.9

haber (future subjunctive)

	sing.	**plural**
1	hubiere	hubiéremos
2	hubieres	hubiereis
3	hubiere	hubieren

Fig. 7.10

Appendix D:
Recommended Books

Barron's Spanish Verbs
by Christopher Kendris, Ph.D.

A History of the Spanish Language
by Ralph Penny

Merriam-Webster's Spanish-English Dictionary

How To Learn Any Language
by Barry Farber

If You Ain't Got No Grammer...
by Brandon Simpson

Learning Foreign Languages
by Brandon Simpson

A New Reference Grammar of Modern Spanish
by John Butt & Carmen Benjamin

Spanglish: The Making of a New American Language
by Ilan Stavans

Spanish Pronunciation: Theory and Practice
by John B. Dalbor

Spanish Verbs & Essentials of Grammar
by Ina W. Ramboz

Spanish Verb Finder
by Dr. Kenneth P. Theda

Brandon Simpson

Appendix E:
English-Spanish Glossary

accent	acento
adjective	adjetivo
aspect	aspecto
clause	cláusula
definite article	artículo definido
dependent	dependiente
direct object	objeto directo
future perfect subjunctive	futuro perfecto de subjuntivo
future subjunctive	futuro de subjuntivo
gerund	gerundio
imperfect	imperfecto
imperfect progressive	imperfecto progresivo
imperfect subjunctive	imperfecto de subjuntivo
imperfective	imperfectivo
indefinite article	artículo indefinido
independent	independiente
indicative	indicativo
indirect object	objeto indirecto
infinitive	infinitivo
main	principal
mood	modo
noun	sustantivo
past infinitive	infinitivo pasado
past participle	participio pasado
past perfect subjunctive	pluscuamperfecto de subjuntivo
perfect	perfecto
perfective	perfectivo
pluperfect	pluscuamperfecto de indicativo
predicate	predicado
present indicative	presente de indicativo
present participle	participio presente
present perfect subjunctive	presente perfecto de subjuntivo
present progressive	presente progresivo
present subjunctive	presente de subjuntivo
preterit	pretérito

preterit progressive	pretérito progresivo
progressive	progresivo
subject	sujeto
subjunctive	subjuntivo
subordinate	subordinado
syllable	sílaba
tense	tiempo
verb	verbo

Appenidx F:
Contact Information

Readers of this book can contact me at **brandonwsimpson@gmail.com** or through social networking sites such as MySpace and YouTube. Go to the following URLs*:

www.BrandonSimpson.net

My MySpace Profile:
http://www.myspace.com/brandonwsimpson

My Group for Foreign Language Enthusiasts:
http://groups.myspace.com/ForeignLanguageEnthusiasts

My YouTube Profile:
http://www.youtube.com/brandonwsimpson

*These could disappear at anytime.

Bibliography

Butt, John and Carmen Benjamin. <u>A New Reference Grammar of Modern Spanish</u>. 3rd ed.Chicago: NTC Publishing Group, 2000.

Dalbor, John B. <u>Spanish Pronunciation: Theory and Practice</u>. 3rd. ed.
Boston: Thomson-Heinle, 1997.

Serrano, Juan and Susan Serrano. <u>Spanish Verbs: Ser and Estar: Key to Mastering the Language</u>. New York: Hippocrene Books, 1992.

Simpson, Brandon. <u>Learning Foreign Languages</u>. Dry Ridge: Small Town P, 2008.

Index

Version History

1.0 March 17, 2008

1.1 June 2, 2008

1.2 September 12, 2008

CPSIA information can be obtained at www.ICGtesting.com
Printed in the USA
BVOW030944260613

324347BV00001B/245/P